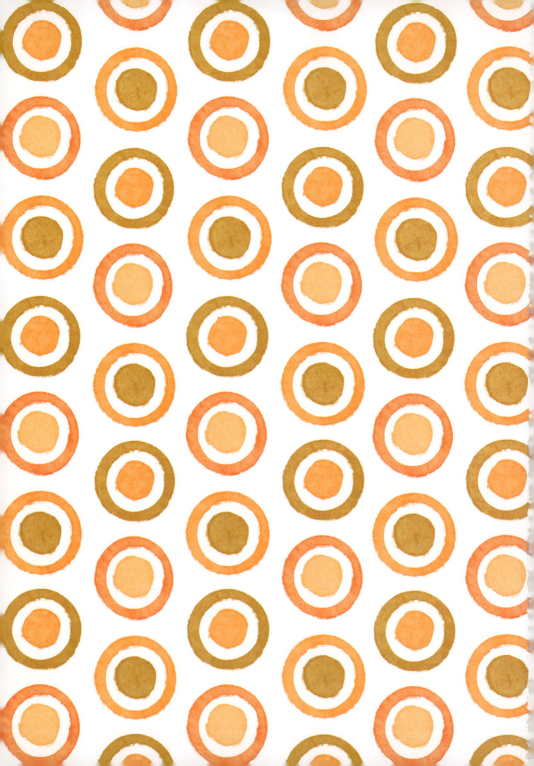

TO

_____

FROM

_____

DATE

_____

HI THERE, FRIEND!

My name is Allyson Golden and I am the founder of Words Are Golden and author of this inspirational and creative journal. I am so happy that this journal has found you wherever you are at today!

A huge passion of mine is to use words to encourage and uplift other women in their identity in Christ. I pray that as you navigate through this journal the Lord would illuminate your mind to see words that we use every day in a new way. My hope for you is that as you discover new truths you would then go and speak that truth over others. Your words hold so much power, and when rooted in the Word of God that holds the ultimate power, your words can change the world.

Sister, our words are **GOLDEN!**

Words Are Golden

ALLYSON GOLDEN

AN INSPIRATIONAL JOURNAL

DaySpring

LIVE YOUR FAITH

Radiant

Those who look to him are radiant, and their faces shall never be ashamed.

PSALM 34:5 ESV

TO BE RADIANT IS TO SHINE BRIGHT.

When God gave us the gift of His son Jesus, He gifted us the light of the world. We are told in I John 1:5 that God is light and in Him there is no darkness at all. Although the world we live in can feel very dark, in Christ there is absolutely no trace of darkness. Then when we look at the book of Genesis, from the beginning, God created us in His image. That means the light of the world lives inside of us! What a privilege it is to be a light carrier. The One who loves us, guides us, strengthens us, and lives in us shines on us and through us. When we look to God, when we place our trust in Him, and when we do our best to become more like Him, we become radiant.

What does it mean to be radiant?

_____

_____

_____

_____

_____

_____

What are ways you can be radiant today? List three below:

_____

_____

_____

_____

_____

Who is someone in your life you think of as radiant?
What characteristics make you think that?
Reach out to them today and tell them they are radiant!

_____

_____

_____

_____

What does it mean to be made in the image of God?
(See Genesis 1:27 for further study.)

_____

_____

_____

_____

_____

"THOSE WHO
LOOK TO HIM
ARE
Radiant"

PSALM 34:5

Challenge: Write a prayer below and use the word radiant in it.

Rejoice in the Lord always; again I will say, rejoice.

PHILIPPIANS 4:4 ESV

TO REJOICE IS TO GIVE JOY TO SOMEONE OR SOMETHING.

We are called to rejoice in the Lord always, so what does that mean? It means to continually find joy in and shout for joy to Him. To rejoice is a choice we get to make. A choice we are called to make whether rejoicing feels hard or easy. But in Nehemiah 8:10 we are told that the joy of the Lord is our strength. When we choose to be joyful in the Lord, He strengthens us and upholds us through times of despair, grief, and struggle. In the midst of hardship, it can seem impossible to have even a glimpse of joy. When we choose to take joy in the Lord for all He has done for us, He fills us with His supernatural and unending joy. It all comes down to the choice. Make the choice to rejoice. He is so deserving of our continual praise. Shout for joy to Him and He will bring joy to you.

What does it mean to you to rejoice?

Do you find it easy to rejoice in the Lord? Why or why not?

_____

_____

_____

_____

_____

What are ways in which you can practice rejoicing?

_____

_____

_____

_____

Make a list of things you can rejoice about today.

_____

_____

_____

_____

_____

_____

_____

Trace the saying "Rejoice in the Lord" over and over again.

rejoice in the Lord.
rejoice in the Lord.
rejoice in the Lord.
rejoice in the Lord.
rejoice in the Lord.
rejoice in the Lord.
rejoice in the Lord.

Pick a day this week and be aware of moments that you can rejoice in. When you see something beautiful, rejoice. When you wake up, rejoice. When you have a good conversation, rejoice. When you see an act of kindness, rejoice. When you feel joyful, rejoice. When you see a friend, rejoice. When you eat a yummy meal, rejoice. When you have a moment of silence, rejoice. Be aware of the tiny moments around you that are happening. Rejoice and give praise to God for those little moments. It might just be a "I take joy in You, Lord" thought or just a quick little "Thank You, Jesus" in your head. Come back to this page and write down all the sweet little moments you chose to rejoice in.

Seek

Ask, and it will be given to you; seek, and you will find; knock, and it will be opened to you.

MATTHEW 7:7 ESV

TO SEEK MEANS TO TRY TO FIND SOMETHING.

The verse above is so beautiful because it doesn't say "seek, and maybe you will find." It says seek and you WILL find. When we search for God, when we seek to know Him with all of our heart, we will find Him. He will meet us when we desire to meet with Him. From the beginning of our lives, He is chasing after our hearts. He wants us to find Him, He wants to reveal Himself to us. He is the kind of God who will never stop chasing after us, even if we stop chasing after Him. But when we choose to seek, when we choose to look for Him, He will be there. Sometimes it may not feel like He is there. Sometimes if we start to seek, we may question where God is. But the thing is, it isn't about a feeling that God is with us, it is the fact that He is with us because He says He is. It may not be some type of grand reveal or crazy feeling but rather just a simple sense of peace in our hearts and minds. He is a God who stays true to His word. So, my friend, seek after Him, you will find Him, and He will be with you every step of the way.

What does the word seek mean to you?

Does seeking to be with Jesus excite you or scare you? Why?

Have you ever lost something, gone looking for it, and found it?
What types of feelings did you have when you found it?
Think of the way Jesus feels when we seek Him and find Him.
What do you think He feels?

What is a way you can incorporate seeking to know Jesus
more in your life?

Look up the four verses and write each of them in the space below.

Matthew 6:33

Matthew 7:8

psalm 27:8

psalm 77:2

Set aside time this week to seek the Lord. Try reading a full chapter of the Bible. If you don't know what to read, try Matthew 7. Listen to a worship song. Journal a prayer. Sit in silence and talk to Jesus. Tell Him your thoughts and feelings. Seek to be with Him. Meet with Him. Write below what that process was like for you.

Victory

The LORD your God is the one who goes with you to fight for you against your enemies to give you victory.

DEUTERONOMY 20:4 NIV

THE MEANING OF THE WORD VICTORY IS SO BEAUTIFUL. IT MEANS TO OVERCOME AN ENEMY.

We know the end of the story, and our God wins. We have the assurance of victory because we know the One who has already overcome it all. How refreshing is that? I think it is something that we can often forget when we want to be the ones in control of our own battles. When we have battles ahead of us or if we are currently in a battle, it is already declared victorious with Jesus. The Lord goes before us and fights for us, we need only to be still. There is no battle that the Lord has ever lost and there isn't a battle that He ever will lose. Victory can be hard to see sometimes. Victory can look different than what we think it will or expect it to. But one thing that is certain is that we do not have to try to fight our battles in our own strength. It is impossible. It is with the strength of Christ and trusting in Him that our battles are won and named victorious.

What does victory mean to you?

Are you in a battle right now? Have you recently come out of a battle? What is it or what was it like?

_____

_____

_____

_____

_____

_____

Is it hard for you to let go of control and let God fight for you? Why or why not?

_____

_____

_____

_____

_____

Every victory matters. Even the tiny victories. What are some victories you have seen in your life?

_____

_____

_____

_____

_____

_____

On the left side underneath "Let Go," write down what you want to let go of, and on the right side underneath "Let God," write down how God names what you are letting go of victorious.

let Go:

let God:

ex: control of my job

ex: my job is in the hand of christ.

1.

2.

3.

4.

5.

In the space below, take the time to write the battles in your life that you are facing right now. Next to each one of them write, Jesus, You have already gone before me, and I hand this battle over to You.

_____

_____

_____

_____

_____

_____

_____

_____

_____

_____

_____

_____

_____

_____

_____

_____

_____

_____

_____

_____

_____

_____

_____

Rooted

So then, just as you received Christ Jesus as Lord, continue to live your lives in Him, rooted and built up in Him, strengthened in the faith as you were taught, and overflowing with thankfulness.

COLOSSIANS 2:6-7 NIV

TO TAKE ROOT OR BE ROOTED IS THE ACT OF ATTACHING TO SOMETHING ELSE OR BECOMING ANCHORED.

So, what does it mean to be rooted in Christ? It means we are anchored to Him and secured to Him. He is our rock. He is our foundation. His characteristics are what we base our lives on. As we learn more about His character and take root in Him, we bloom into the children of God He has made us to be. We are to live a life that is "rooted and built up in Him." Think of a flower that is potted in good soil—its roots flourish and grow deep, and the flowers bloom in abundance. When our roots are growing in the good soil of who Christ is, they grow deep and strong and we bloom in abundance. As we continue our walk with Him, our roots grow deeper and deeper in His love, grace, mercy, joy, and abundance.

What does it mean to you to be rooted in Christ?

_____

_____

_____

What are some of your favorite characteristics of Christ?
List them below.

_____

_____

_____

_____

_____

_____

Where do you find your roots planted right now? Are they growing
in Christ? Or are they planted in the things of this world?

_____

_____

_____

_____

_____

Is there someone in your life who is deeply rooted in Christ?
What makes you think that or know that about them?

_____

_____

_____

_____

_____

_____

Along each of the roots, write the characteristics of Christ you want to be rooted in.

love

Read this passage and meditate on it:

For this reason I kneel before the Father, from whom every family in heaven and on earth derives its name. I pray that out of His glorious riches He may strengthen you with power through His Spirit in your inner being, so that Christ may dwell in your hearts through faith. And I pray that you, being rooted and established in love, may have power, together with all the Lord's holy people, to grasp how wide and long and high and deep is the love of Christ, and to know this love that surpasses knowledge—that you may be filled to the measure of all the fullness of God.

—Ephesians 3:14–19 NIV

Journal below what these verses mean to you.

grace

By grace you have been saved through faith. And this is not your own doing; it is the gift of God, not a result of works, so that no one may boast.

EPHESIANS 2:8-9 ESV

BIBLICAL GRACE IS DEFINED AS BEING SET FREE FROM SIN THROUGH DIVINE ASSISTANCE.

It is by the grace of God that we are set free from our sins. God's grace is one of the most beautiful gifts that is given to us. We are not deserving of this grace, but because of who He is, it is freely given to us. Grace can be a word that we throw around here and there, but the meaning of this word is truly incredible. Grace is freedom. Grace is what gives us eternal life. Grace is what makes us kneel at the feet of Jesus. Grace sustains us. Grace is who Jesus is. It gives us every reason to praise and give thanks to God for the fact that He just hands it to us because He loves us. He sees us as His children, in need and desperate for grace, and He holds it out to us as a sweet gift. There is nothing we have to do to earn this grace. There is nothing we can do to be "more" deserving of this grace. He wants us to simply accept it. Accepting all of who He is and the grace that He has for us is the best thing we could ever do.

What does "saved by grace" mean to you?

_____

_____

_____

_____

Where in your life have you experienced God's grace?

_____

_____

_____

_____

Have you ever felt like you needed to do something in order to earn God's grace?

_____

_____

_____

_____

What does it feel like to be given something that we are undeserving of yet so freely given?

_____

_____

_____

_____

"But because of His GREAT love for us, God, who is rich in mercy, made us alive with Christ even when we were dead in transgressions— it is by GRACE you have been saved."

EPHESIANS 2:4-5

Write a prayer of thanks to God for His never-ending grace.

Bask

He makes me lie down in green pastures, He leads me beside quiet waters, He refreshes my soul.

PSALM 23:2–3 NIV

TO BASK IS TO LIE DOWN OR RELAX, ENJOYING THE WARMTH OF THE SUN OR A PLEASANT ATMOSPHERE.

God desires for us to lie down and be refreshed and renewed by Him. He wants us to be still so that He can speak His truth over us and overwhelm us with His presence. It can be hard to slow down in this fast-paced world, but there is so much to be seen in the slow and steady. When we are always on the go and always thinking about what is next for us, it can be difficult to hear what God is wanting to say to us. Think about a green pasture. It is a place of peace, a place of quiet, a place of tranquility. Now think about a beautiful lake or a large pond. The water is so still, so calm. This psalm conjures up images of such beautiful and peaceful places to show us the peace He wants to provide us with. He truly just wants to be with us. He wants us to bask in His love. He wants us to bask in His grace. He wants us to bask in His peace. He wants us to bask in all that He is.

What does it mean to you to "bask in His love"?

Picture the most peaceful place you have ever been or experienced. Write about it below.

_____

_____

_____

_____

_____

Is it easy or hard for you to slow down and rest? Why do you think that is?

_____

_____

_____

_____

_____

What do you think is the difference between spiritual rest and physical rest?

_____

_____

_____

_____

_____

_____

In the space below, draw a peaceful place:

my place of peace:

Take ten to twenty minutes to sit in complete silence.
No music, no podcasts, just you and God. Write about the time
basking in His presence.

Flourish

I am like a flourishing olive tree in the house of God; I trust in God's faithful love forever and ever.

PSALM 52:8 CSB

TO FLOURISH IS TO GROW IN ABUNDANCE, TO THRIVE.

So what does it mean to flourish like an olive tree in the house of God? It means to be rooted in Christ and strengthened by His living water. An olive tree is a symbol of peace, so to flourish is to grow abundantly in His peace and in who He is. Flourishing isn't something that just happens in an instant, though; it is a growing process. Just like any type of growth, it takes time and discipline. To flourish in Christ is to get to know who He is. It is taking the time to read His Word, spending time in prayer and talking to Him, and just enjoying time in His presence. Flourishing in Christ is very different from trying to flourish in the world. To be flourishing in the world is to be successful and productive. Flourishing in Christ takes slowing down, being with Him, and learning about Him. As we grow and root ourselves in who He is, the abundant life that He promises us becomes more evident. He desires for us to have abundant life in Him. He wants us to be flourishing in Him. Just as a flower needs light and water to flourish, we too need His light and His living water to grow in abundance.

What does it mean to you to flourish in Christ?

What does it mean to be flourishing in the world? How does that differ from flourishing in Christ?

Do you know someone who is flourishing in the Lord? What makes you think that about them?

What is a step you can take today to flourish more in the Lord?

A way to study God's Word more in-depth is to look at multiple Bible translations. Look up four or five different Bible translations of the verse below and write them in the free space:

John 10:10

Write down some ways in which you are trying to flourish in the world. Write down ways you can start to flourish more in the Lord. Then write a little prayer surrendering the things of the world to Him.

Wait

But they who wait for the Lord shall renew their strength; they shall mount up with wings like eagles; they shall run and not be weary; they shall walk and not faint.

ISAIAH 40:31 ESV

TO WAIT IS TO BE IN EXPECTATION OF SOMETHING HAPPENING.

Waiting is hard, especially when we want something to happen right away. Waiting seasons can be challenging. They allow us to trust in God's timing. When we wait on the Lord, our strength is renewed. His Spirit dwells in us, and we are able to run the race set before us even if we aren't quite sure what it looks like. The Lord is always at work for our good, and we can trust in Him in our waiting. When we draw near to God, He draws near to us. He shows us in His perfect timing what is next. He reveals to us the yes or the no, knowing what is best for us and delivering it to us. God is on our side and fights on our behalf for us. We can have peace and contentment in the waiting knowing that it is for our good and that it is full of the love that the Lord has for us. Let the love of the Lord strengthen you in your waiting!

What does it mean to you to wait?

Are you in a waiting season now? What is it? If you aren't, what is one you have been in before?

What has been the outcome of a past waiting season?

What makes waiting so hard? How can we work on learning to trust during the waiting seasons we face?

"they who wait on the Lord shall renew their strength; they shall mount up with wings like eagles; they shall run and not be weary; they shall walk and not faint."

Isaiah 40:31

Journal below about a waiting season you have been through and where you saw God in it. How was it hard to see Him in it? Do you now see the purpose of that season? Jot down your thoughts in the space below; find where God was in your waiting.

Redeemed

Christ redeemed us from that self-defeating, cursed life by absorbing it completely into Himself. Do you remember the Scripture that says, "Cursed is everyone who hangs on a tree"? That is what happened when Jesus was nailed to the cross: He became a curse, and at the same time dissolved the curse. And now, because of that, the air is cleared and we can see that Abraham's blessing is present and available for non-Jews, too. We are all able to receive God's life, His Spirit, in and with us by believing—just the way Abraham received it.

GALATIANS 3:13-14 THE MESSAGE

TO BE REDEEMED IS TO BE SET FREE FROM THE CONSEQUENCES OF SIN.

It is by the act of Jesus dying on the cross for our sins that we have been set free. It is the greatest act of love ever done. By Him and in Him we are redeemed. When we say yes to Jesus, we are washed white as snow. All the sins of our past are wiped clean. As we move forward and strive to not sin, we are covered by His grace. He is the ultimate redeemer, and His redemption is available for every single person. He doesn't redeem just for a select few, for those that "do good," or for specific groups. No, He is for every single human on the earth. He wants to set every one of His children free. He wants people to experience the love, peace, grace, and redemption that He freely gives to us.

What does it mean to you to be redeemed?

_____

_____

_____

_____

We are imperfect people living in an imperfect world.
How does redemption come into play even when we still sin
after saying yes to Jesus?

_____

_____

_____

_____

What does redemption teach you about the cross?

_____

_____

_____

_____

What are ways you can live fully in your redemption today?

_____

_____

_____

Trace the saying "He is my redeemer" over and over.
Hold that truth in your heart today.

He is my redeemer

He is my redeemer

He is my redeemer

He is my redeemer

He is my redeemer

He is my redeemer

Write to God and thank Him for Jesus' redemption on the cross.
As you write, listen for how God wants to speak to you.

Persevere

Blessed is the one who perseveres under trial because, having stood the test, that person will receive the crown of life that the Lord has promised to those who love Him.

JAMES 1:12 NIV

TO PERSEVERE IS TO MAINTAIN A PURPOSE IN SPITE OF DIFFICULTY, OBSTACLES, OR DISCOURAGEMENT AND TO CONTINUE ON STEADFASTLY.

We are told in the Bible that we are going to have trials here on this earth. This life we live is going to have hardships, and it isn't going to be painless. It is easy to have a mindset that life as a Christian will be easy. Unfortunately, that isn't true. Although it isn't going to be easy, it is going to be way more than worth it in the end to push through the hardships because we are promised the crown of life. We aren't alone in our trials. Jesus withstood many trials here on earth. If there is anyone who knows how hard it is to stand up for what you know is right and true, it is Him. And He is living inside of us! The same Spirit who raised Jesus from the grave, the same Spirit who lived in Jesus as He walked the earth, is living inside of us. Through Christ and in Christ we have His strength to help us persevere through all the trials and hardships we will face here on earth.

What does it mean to you to persevere?

_____

_____

_____

_____

What are some trials you have had to persevere through?

_____

_____

_____

_____

_____

Looking back on those trials, how was God at work through them?

_____

_____

_____

_____

When we are told we are promised the crown of life after persevering through our trials here on earth, what does that mean to you?

_____

_____

_____

_____

_____

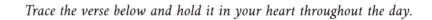

Trace the verse below and hold it in your heart throughout the day.

"We glory in our
sufferings, because
we know that suffering
produces perseverance;
perseverance, character;
and character, hope."

Romans 5:3-4

Write the verse from the activity on the previous page on a
sticky note or a piece of paper and tape it to your bathroom mirror.
Read the verse every time you brush your teeth or get ready this week.
Come back and journal about the experience.

You make known to me the path of life; you will fill me with joy in Your presence, with eternal pleasures at Your right hand.

PSALM 16:11 NIV

THE DEFINITION OF JOY IN A DICTIONARY INDICATES A FEELING OF PLEASURE OR HAPPINESS, BUT TRUE JOY IN THE LORD IS SO MUCH MORE THAN THAT.

Joy is more of an experience than a feeling. It comes from experiencing the real, tangible presence of God. In the presence of the Lord there is fullness of joy, as we read in the verse above. We find joy in Him that is unexplainable. It can be easy in this world to want to chase after things that we think will make us feel happy or feel this sense of joy, only to find they leave us empty or only happy for a short time. That is because we look to things that are temporary to make us feel what we are deeply searching for. That thing we are searching for is true joy in the Lord, and that comes when we sit in His presence and learn about His character. It is easy to feel like joy is impossible when the circumstances or challenges we face are hard and seem unbearable. But even in the hurting and hardship, joy is attainable because the presence of the Lord is constant. The more we learn about Him, the more we take joy in who He is and what is promised to us. He wants to fill us with unexplainable and unimaginable joy; we only need to sit in His presence.

What does joy in the Lord mean to you?

_____

_____

_____

_____

Have you looked to earthly things to fill you with a sense of happiness? How did that end and what have you learned from it?

_____

_____

_____

_____

What do you feel is the difference between happiness and joy?

_____

_____

_____

_____

Has there been a time in your life when you experienced the joy of the Lord? Write about it below.

_____

_____

_____

_____

Look up these verses and write them in the areas below:

Romans 15:13

Acts 2:28

Pick three friends and text them this verse:

"You make known to me the path of life; you will fill me with joy in your presence, with eternal pleasures at your right hand."

—Psalm 16:11

Encourage them that the joy of the Lord is their strength. Write about that experience and their responses below.

Abide

Abide in me, and I in you. As the branch cannot bear fruit by itself, unless it abides in the vine, neither can you, unless you abide in me.

JOHN 15:4 ESV

THE DEFINITION OF ABIDE IS TO REMAIN IN OR TO STAY.

In the verse above, Jesus asks us to abide in Him as He abides in us. He then gives us a beautiful example of a plant that bears and produces fruit. This verse shows us that in order for us to grow, we must abide in Him. In order for us to go and be His hands and feet and bring others to know who He is, we must spend time with Him. This verse is beautiful not just because Jesus calls us to be with Him but because He is telling us that He is with us, He is in us, and He will never leave us. He is where we get our strength, joy, endurance, and energy to live a life that produces great fruit. This fruit refers to the things that come from our lives. It is not in our own strength that we can be successful in living out our calling. It is through abiding in Jesus and resting all that we are in Him that we can live a life of peace and true freedom. As we abide in Him, He promises to abide in us.

What does it mean to you to abide in the Lord?

Where do you feel you get your strength, energy, and endurance from? Are you looking to the world to sustain you or to the Lord?

When you hear "a branch cannot bear fruit by itself," what does that mean to you?

What do you feel when you hear that as we abide in Jesus He abides in us also?

Trace the verse below and try to memorize it:

"Abide in me, and I in you."

John 15:4

What is an area in your life that you have been trying to control in your own strength? How can you begin to abide in the Lord in that area? Journal about it below.

Light

Again Jesus spoke to them, saying, "I am the light of the world. Whoever follows me will not walk in darkness, but will have the light of life."

JOHN 8:12 ESV

LIGHT IS WHAT MAKES THINGS VISIBLE. IT CAN ALSO BE DEFINED AS SOMETHING SHINING.

In the verse above, we see Jesus calling Himself the light. He defines Himself as the shining one. It can be really hard to remember this quality about Jesus, especially when we feel surrounded by the darkness of the world or even the darkness that we partake in as sinners. But when we say yes to Jesus and choose to follow Him, we no longer walk in darkness. His guiding light is leading us and is with us. His light is within us as His Spirit is within us. We have the shining light of Christ alive inside of us! It is always there, shining through the dark; it just takes remembering and recognizing that the light truly is there. It isn't something made up; it isn't a dream. Jesus tells us that He is the light and that as we walk with Him we will have the light of life. We must remind ourselves that His light truly is always alive! Though there is darkness in the world, the darkness has already been overcome by the light who overcame the world. He is our shining light, and we get to go out and reflect who He is to the world through the way we love, forgive, act, and live. He is always with us. He is always ready to shine through us.

What does light mean to you?

_____

_____

_____

_____

What does it mean to you when you hear Jesus is the light of the world?

_____

_____

_____

_____

Is it hard for you to see past the darkness in this world and in your life?

_____

_____

_____

_____

What are ways in which you can be a light for Christ?

_____

_____

_____

_____

Trace the verse below and then send it to a friend to encourage them:

"the light shines
in the darkness
and the darkness
has not overcome
it"

john 1:5

Who is someone in your life who shines bright or truly reflects who Jesus is? Write them a text or a little card and encourage them in that. Journal below about that experience and about the ways that you can go out and be a light for Christ today.

Known

You have searched me, LORD, and you know me. You know when I sit and when I rise; You perceive my thoughts from afar. You discern my going out and my lying down; You are familiar with all my ways.

PSALM 139:1-3 NIV

TO BE KNOWN IS TO UNDERSTAND SOMETHING OR TO HAVE INFORMATION ABOUT SOMETHING.

God fully understands us, and God is aware of every single thing about us. We are deeply known by God. He sees us right where we are, knows every detail of our life, and chooses to love us. This world can easily make us feel isolated. Social media has a big impact on making us feel alone or unknown. We see our friends together but we weren't invited. We pick and choose what we want others to know about us, leaving us feeling empty and lonely. We long to feel known by others, which truly is important, but we easily forget how deeply known we are by the Lord. We look to the things of this world to try to feel known and are never satisfied. But the Bible tells us that the Lord fully knows us. He knows where we have been, He knows where we are, and He knows where we are going. He knows what makes us smile, He knows what upsets us, and He knows the deepest desires and longings of our heart. He wants to show us how truly known we are by Him. He wants to lavish His love on us by knowing us specifically. He formed us in our mothers' wombs, knew us by name before our parents gave us a name, and sees us for who we truly are. In Him we are fully known and fully loved.

What does it mean to you to be known?

_____

_____

_____

_____

Do you find yourself looking to things of this world to feel known? What things do you look to? Do they make you feel truly known?

_____

_____

_____

_____

Do you ever feel like there are things you can hide from God or things He doesn't know about?

_____

_____

_____

_____

When you read about how known you truly are, how did it make you feel?

_____

_____

_____

_____

fully known + fully loved
fully known + fully loved
fully known + fully loved
fully known + fully loved
fully known + fully loved
fully known + fully loved
fully known + fully loved

Who is someone who has made you feel known?
Reach out to them and thank them for making you feel that way.
Journal about the experience below.

Legacy

I call to God Most High, to God who fulfills His purpose for me.

PSALM 57:2 CSB

A LEGACY IS SOMETHING THAT IS HANDED DOWN.

Legacy is the way that someone lives their life and how their life impacts those around them. When it comes to the life you are living, how is it impacting your family? Is it something you are proud of? What are you going to be remembered by? The answers to those questions are all a part of the legacy you are living out right now. Are you trying to live by your own rules, needs, and wants? Or are you trying to live by the guidance of the Lord, trusting Him with your life and living by His example? We have the choice to walk in our God-given purpose or in a way that is dictated by what we want. The Lord has established our purpose from the very beginning. He created us in our mothers' womb to live on this earth for a specific reason. It is hard to know what that specific reason is, but we can trust that as long as we are following Jesus all the days of our life, that reason and purpose will be fulfilled. Living a life following the Lord isn't going to be glamorous or easy, but it will be fulfilling and there will be an eternal reward at the end. What is the legacy that you want to leave behind?

What does the word legacy mean to you?

_____

_____

_____

_____

When you hear the question "What is the legacy you are leaving behind?" what feelings or thoughts does it bring up?

_____

_____

_____

_____

What is one step you can make today to better the legacy you are leaving behind?

_____

_____

_____

_____

In your own words, what is the legacy that Jesus lived and left behind for us?

_____

_____

_____

_____

Someone who left behind a great legacy :

what made their legacy so great?

where do you see jesus in their legacy ?

Write about the legacy you want to leave behind.

Original

Since this is the kind of life we have chosen, the life of the Spirit, let us make sure that we do not just hold it as an idea in our heads or a sentiment in our hearts, but work out its implications in every detail of our lives. That means we will not compare ourselves with each other as if one of us were better and another worse. We have far more interesting things to do with our lives. Each of us is an original.

GALATIANS 5:25–26 THE MESSAGE

TO BE ORIGINAL IS TO BE MADE NEW, TO BE MADE FOR THE FIRST TIME.

We are each an original human. There has never been anyone exactly like us, and there never will be. We are God's true and original design. It is so easy to wish we were made differently or that we had the qualities of another. But the thing is, God placed His special gifts within us for the world to experience. He made us each unique and original because He chose us to live out the distinct calling He has placed on our lives. He didn't create you to come and live out the life He has planned for another. No, He made you to live out the beautiful life He has planned for you. It's easy to get caught in the trap of wanting what others have and striving to be "someone" or to be "successful" in this world. But part of being an original means we have our very own success story that looks nothing like our neighbor's. God calls us to walk in His truth, His light, and His calling on our lives. Where He calls is better than any place we could get to on our own. His plan from the beginning was for us to live out His original plan for our lives. You are an original, so walk in that identity today.

What does original mean to you?

_____

_____

_____

_____

We are told in the Bible that we are God's original design.
Is it hard for you to believe that or easy?

_____

_____

_____

_____

Do you ever have thoughts of wishing you were someone else?
What do you think sparks those thoughts?

_____

_____

_____

_____

What thoughts and feelings do you have toward the fact that God
made us each original?

_____

_____

_____

_____

Trace over the design below, and in the blank puzzle spaces write what makes you original:

I am an ORIGINAL design

Make a list of things that you feel God has uniquely placed within you. Thank Him for each of those things, and ask Him how you can work to use those gifts to glorify Him.

Endure

Consider him who endured from sinners such hostility against himself, so that you may not grow weary or fainthearted.

HEBREWS 12:3 ESV

TO ENDURE SOMETHING IS TO HOLD OUT WITHOUT GIVING UP.

Jesus is the greatest example of someone who endured. He endured persecution. He endured hate. He endured suffering. He endured the cross. We are also called to endure. It's easy to think that following Jesus would make life easier, but in fact God promised us we would have troubles (John 16:33). After all, we are living in a fallen world, and there is no getting away from the suffering. But there is a way to endure the suffering and persecution that come with living on this earth and being a follower of Jesus. He modeled for us what it looks like to endure hardship, and we too can do it. The same Spirit that gave Jesus the strength to endure what He went through and raised Him from the dead lives within us. We are strengthened by Christ and upheld by Him, and He helps us persevere through the trials that come our way so that we can give glory to His name. We do not need to be discouraged by hardships because the Lord is with us and will help us endure.

What does it mean to you to endure?

_____

_____

_____

_____

What hardships have you had to endure in your life?

_____

_____

_____

_____

How has God carried you through those hardships?

_____

_____

_____

_____

Jesus modeled what it means to endure. What does that mean to you?

_____

_____

_____

_____

"BUT IF YOU ENDURE
STEADFASTLY WHEN
YOU'VE DONE GOOD
AND SUFFER FOR IT,
THIS IS COMMENDABLE
BEFORE GOD."

1 PETER 2:20 CEB

WHAT DOES THIS VERSE MEAN?

Write about a hardship or time of suffering from your past. Looking back, where do you see God at work? How did He bring you through? Then thank Him for that time and how He was truly with you all along.

Courageous

Haven't I commanded you: be strong and courageous?
Do not be afraid or discouraged, for the LORD your God
is with you wherever you go.

JOSHUA 1:9 CSB

TO BE COURAGEOUS IS TO FACE DIFFICULTY WITHOUT FEAR.

We are told in the Bible that we are going to face difficulty in this world, but Jesus tells us to take heart because He has already overcome the world (John 16:33). Yet it is still hard to be courageous in this world that is filled with hurt, darkness, and hardship. But the Lord tells us that we do not need to be afraid or discouraged because He is always with us. Not only is He always with us, but He has gone before us! He already knows each of the difficulties and hardships that will come our way, and He knows we can overcome them with His help. He is our overcomer, and it is only with Him that we can be courageous. If we tried to be courageous in our own strength, we would fall into the trap of fear. But when we stand strong and courageous in the Lord and cast all our fears on Him, He equips us with exactly what we need to fight our battles. When Jesus was on earth, He modeled for us what it means to truly be courageous and face difficulty without fear. He was able to do so because He knew where His treasure was: in heaven. He knew He had nothing to fear in the grand scheme of things. The same goes for us. We do not need to fear because our God is with us, for us, and in us! We can be courageous in the strength of the Lord!

What does it mean to you to be courageous?

Has there been a time in your life when you had to choose to be courageous? Write about it.

When it comes to facing difficulties, what fears usually arise within you?

What makes it hard for you to be courageous? What are things that motivate you to be courageous?

A TIME IN YOUR LIFE IN WHICH YOU FELT COURAGEOUS:

WHAT MADE YOU FEEL COURAGEOUS?

WHERE DO YOU SEE GOD IN THAT SITUATION?

Choose to do something courageous today. Reach out to someone you have been thinking of. Forgive someone you need to forgive. Make a baby step toward a dream. Reach out and tell someone about something you've been holding onto. Take one courageous step today and journal about it below.

Surrender

He was saying to them all, "If anyone wishes to follow Me [as My disciple], *he must deny himself* [set aside selfish interests], *and take up his cross daily* [expressing a willingness to endure whatever may come] *and follow Me* [believing in Me, conforming to My example in living and, if need be, suffering or perhaps dying because of faith in Me]."

LUKE 9:23 AMP

TO SURRENDER IS TO GIVE UP ONESELF TO THE POWER OF ANOTHER.

That is exactly what God asks us to do. He simply asks us to surrender all of who we are to Him. He asks us to give up ourselves to His power, His truth, and His authority. While giving up control of our lives may not be easy, it's the only choice that allows us to live with true peace and hope for the future. When we choose to surrender our life to the Lord, it is an act of saying, "Not my will but your will be done." The thing is, His will for us is best, not to mention His plans for our lives are so much better than anything we could ever dream or imagine (Ephesians 3:20). God knows us better than we know ourselves. He put us here on this earth for a purpose, and He wants to fulfill that purpose in us. We cannot do it on our own; we can only do it by the strength of Christ through surrender. As we hand ourselves over to God, He takes care of us with His gentle spirit and loving character. In our surrender there is beauty to be found, hope to be discovered, and miraculous love to be received.

What does surrender mean to you?

Is it hard for you to surrender yourself to the Lord? Why or why not?

What is hardest for you to surrender to the Lord (finances, future, etc.)?

What are ways in which Jesus modeled surrendering while He was here on earth?

Fill in the blanks with things you want or need to surrender to God today:

I Surrender: _____

I Surrender: _____

I Surrender: _____

I Surrender: _____

I Surrender: _____

I Surrender: _____

Journal about an area that is hard for you to fully surrender to the Lord. Ask Him to reveal to you why it is hard for you and to help you have the strength to fully hand it over to Him.

Bloom

The seed that fell among thorns stands for those who hear, but as they go on their way they are choked by life's worries, riches and pleasures, and they do not mature. But the seed on good soil stands for those with a noble and good heart, who hear the word, retain it, and by persevering produce a crop.

LUKE 8:14-15 NIV

TO BLOOM IS TO PRODUCE OR YIELD BLOSSOMS, AND BLOSSOMS ARE THE FLOWER OR FRUIT THAT IS BROUGHT TO FLOURISHING THROUGH THE GROWTH PROCESS.

What determines our growth is the "soil" in which we are planted. Are we digging our roots into superficial and temporary things? Or are we digging our roots into our faith and God's Word? When we dig our roots in good soil, the fruit and blossoms produced are bountiful and beautiful. When a plant has many blooms, it is because of the soil in which it is planted. Being surrounded by rich nutrients (God's truth and Word) enables us to stay strong when storms come or we feel scorched by the sun. What we take in affects what we produce—not in the sense of productivity but the qualities and characteristics evident in our lives. The more we are in the Word of God, the more we bloom into who He has called us to be. The blossoms that form are ones of strength, dignity, humility, love, kindness, and all the characteristics of who God is.

What does it mean to you to bloom?

_____

_____

_____

What kind of soil are you planting yourself in?

_____

_____

_____

What kind of blossoms do you see forming within you?

_____

_____

_____

We are always growing; we are always blooming in some type of way.
But as we grow we face storms and trials. What are some trials you are
facing right now? How is God continuing to strengthen you to grow?

_____

_____

_____

On the lines below, write the areas in which you feel you are blooming:

blooming in:

_____

_____

_____

_____

_____

Think back on the past year of your life. What is a way in which you have bloomed? Journal about it below.

Stillness

Be still, and know that I am God. I will be exalted among the nations, I will be exalted in the earth!

PSALM 46:10 ESV

TO SIT IN STILLNESS IS TO SIT IN THE QUIET OR TO REST.

In the Bible God calls us multiple times to be still and to rest. The Lord desires for us to just sit in His presence so that He can cover us in His love and His grace. In a busy world that makes us feel like we must strive to be somebody or achieve x, y, and z to be loved, it is refreshing that our God just wants us to be still. God doesn't ask us to do certain things in order to be loved by Him. He simply wants us as we are, and He wants to provide us with His sweet presence as we choose to be still with Him. There is such sweetness in stillness. When we can silence the voices of the world and listen in the quiet for His sweet voice, He shows up. He loves to speak to His children. He loves to cover us with His peace. He loves to teach us about His grace and who He is. It can be hard to be fully present with the Lord when we are trying to multitask or thinking about what we have to do next. But He asks us to put aside everything, lay it at His feet, and just be with Him. In His presence there is fullness of joy. In the stillness, the sweet presence of the Lord fills us.

What does stillness mean to you?

Is it challenging for you to sit in stillness? Why or why not?

What does resting in the Lord look like to you?

How do you fight distraction in the stillness?

In the circles below, write the places you feel most at peace.

where do you feel most at peace?

Set aside fifteen minutes and just sit in stillness. No music, no reading, just the quiet and the presence of Lord. Invite His presence into the space and ask Him to speak to you. Journal about the experience below.

Freedom

For you, my brothers, were called to freedom; only do not let your freedom become an opportunity for the sinful nature (worldliness, selfishness), but through love serve and seek the best for one another.

GALATIANS 5:13 AMP

TO BE SET FREE IS TO BE RELEASED FROM BONDAGE.

Jesus came to the earth to set us free. When He died on the cross for our sins, He made it possible for us to experience true forgiveness and release from shame—we no longer have to be tied down by our past mistakes. This is what we call freedom in Christ. It's not the type of freedom where we can do whatever is pleasing to us, but the type that allows us to get back up so that we can love others, serve others, and seek the best for others. Our freedom means going and boasting about who Jesus is and what He has done for us. We are to tell people about the freedom we have experienced in Christ so that they can experience it as well. It is such a beautiful feeling knowing that we aren't tied to our sin or held down by our past. The chains that held us down for so long have been broken, and now we get to walk in freedom with Christ.

What does freedom in Christ mean to you?

_____

_____

_____

Jesus died for your sins so that you could be set free.
How does that make you feel?

How can you walk in that freedom today?

What are some things that make you feel free? What does it feel like
to be free?

Trace the verse below:

"where the spirit of the Lord is there is freedom!"

2 CORINTHIANS 3:17

Name some specific things that Christ has set you free from.
Journal them below and declare the freedom you now have from them.
Thank Him for setting you free.

grit

And not only this, but [with joy] *let us exult in our sufferings and rejoice in our hardships, knowing that hardship* (distress, pressure, trouble) *produces patient endurance; and endurance, proven character* (spiritual maturity); *and proven character, hope and confident assurance* [of eternal salvation].

ROMANS 5:3-4 AMP

TO HAVE GRIT IS TO BE FIRM IN CHARACTER, TO BE COURAGEOUS.

To be someone with grit is to be someone who is firm in their identity in Christ. So firm that no suffering or hardship can knock them all the way down because their strength and identity are fully in Christ. The more hardship and suffering that we face, the stronger we get and the more endurance we build. As our endurance builds, our character becomes firmer in the Lord. To have grit isn't easy. It means that you have been through a good amount of hardship and suffering. But we don't need to worry because we are told that the Lord has already overcome the world. He is in full control. He is leading us on His path of abundance. It takes courage to fully surrender through trials, but the Lord promises us that He will guide us through. And as He guides us on His perfect path, our character forms and we become spiritually mature. We have this hope in Christ that we can hold onto forever. We can have grit as we trust in Him.

What does it mean to you to have grit?

Name a situation in which you needed to have grit.

How did you grow through that situation? What was the end result?

What makes it hard to have grit sometimes?

To be someone
with grit is to be
someone who is
firm in their
identity in Christ.

What is a challenge you have faced recently or are currently facing?
How can you choose to have grit in the situation?

Meek

Put on then, as God's chosen ones, holy and beloved, compassionate hearts, kindness, humility, meekness, and patience, bearing with one another and, if one has a complaint against another, forgiving each other; as the Lord has forgiven you, so you also must forgive.

COLOSSIANS 3:12-13 ESV

TO BE MEEK IS TO BE HUMBLY PATIENT, QUIET IN NATURE, GENTLE, AND KIND.

Meekness is a quality that we are asked to walk in, but one that can be very hard and testing. Often, our first instinct isn't to be meek. When someone wrongs us, choosing to be patient, gentle, and kind is the last thing that our human flesh wants to do. It can be hard to even know how to be meek to those who hurt us or persecute us. Lucky for us, though, Jesus lived a beautiful life embodying what it is to be meek. When He was persecuted, He chose gentleness. When others wronged Him, He chose kindness. And when others went against Him, He was patient. To walk in meekness is to choose to walk like Jesus did. It's not going to be easy. Jesus didn't live an easy life, but He did live one that was very meaningful. The way He lived impacted others. How He responded to things truly affected those around Him. The same can be true for us when we choose to be meek.

What does it mean to you to be meek?

_____

_____

What makes it hard to put on meekness?

_____

_____

_____

_____

_____

What inspires you to try to be meek?

_____

_____

_____

_____

_____

Do you know someone personally who embodies the quality of meekness well? What is it about them?

_____

_____

_____

_____

_____

_____

_____

Circle one of the five words below, and in the space underneath write about how you will work on embodying it.

compassion
HUMility KINDNESS
meekness
Patience

_____

Be aware this week of opportunities to choose to be meek.
Whether someone wrongs you, hurts you, or causes you to feel impatient,
try to respond with a heart that is meek. Journal about the experience
below. Was it easy to respond in that way? Why or why not?

Peacemaker

Blessed are the peacemakers, for they will be called children of God.

MATTHEW 5:9 NIV

A PEACEMAKER IS SOMEONE WHO IS ACTIVELY TRYING TO RECONCILE PEOPLE TO ONE OTHER AND TO GOD.

Being a peacemaker is very challenging, especially when you feel the need to fight for what you know to be right. But Jesus came so that we would have peace, and that means walking and living in peace with one another. Our problems with other people aren't going to just go away; it takes work. It takes knowing that it ultimately doesn't matter here on earth whether we are right or wrong about one little thing. What matters is living in peace and harmony with one another and chasing the heart of God together. A peacemaker is someone who puts the needs of others before their own. The Bible says that those who seek peace will be called children of God. We are called in the Bible to live at peace with one another—and in doing so, the God of all peace will be with us.

What does being a peacemaker mean to you?

_____

_____

_____

_____

When you hear that God is peace, what does that mean to you and how does it make you feel?

_____

_____

_____

_____

_____

What does it feel like to not have peace in the relationships around you?

_____

_____

_____

_____

_____

What does peace feel like to you?

_____

_____

_____

_____

_____

_____

Trace the verse below:

"Do all that
you can
to live
in peace
with one
another."

Romans 12:18

Write down the name of someone you need to make peace with. What is it you need to make peace with them about? Why has it been hard to do so? Know that the God of peace is with you, and if you feel the tug and call on your heart, then go and make peace with them.

Wonder

I will establish your descendants as kings forever; they will sit on your throne from now until eternity. All heaven will praise Your great wonders, Lord; myriads of angels will praise You for Your faithfulness. For who in all of heaven can compare with the Lord? What mightiest angel is anything like the Lord?

PSALM 89:4-6 NLT

WONDER IS A CAUSE OF ASTONISHMENT.

God is the God of wonder. He is astonishing. There aren't enough words to describe how amazing He truly is. When Jesus was on earth, He performed many miracles and wonders. The things that He did left people in awe and amazement. The wonder of the Lord is what makes Him higher than all. No one can compare to Him. No one can do what He does. And one of the most beautiful things about God is that He shows us these signs and wonders out of love for us. Because of the marvelous things He has done and will continue to do, we can't help but praise Him all the days of our lives. Picture what it will be like the day you meet the Lord. Not only will He be praised for all the wonders He has performed, but we will stand in front of Him full of wonder and awe.

What does wonder mean to you?

_____

_____

What is one of your favorite acts of wonder Jesus did here on earth?

_____

_____

_____

_____

_____

_____

When you hear about the signs and wonders of God, what does it make you think and feel?

_____

_____

_____

_____

_____

When was a time you felt in awe and wonder? Write about it below.

_____

_____

_____

_____

_____

_____

_____

Trace the quote from Francis of Assisi below:

"The world is a great stage on which God displays His many wonders."

-Francis of Assisi

Listen to your favorite worship song. Write about the wonder you feel as you listen to the song and imagine the day you meet the Lord.

In your hearts honor Christ the Lord as holy, always being prepared to make a defense to anyone who asks you for a reason for the hope that is in you; yet do it with gentleness and respect.

1 PETER 3:15 ESV

TO SHOW HONOR IS TO SHOW RESPECT.

What does living an honorable life look like? What does it truly mean to honor God, and how do we do it? It means we recognize Him for who He is as God above it all. It is respecting who He is because He deserves all the glory and praise. God made the ultimate sacrifice for us when He sent His son Jesus to save us, and that in itself is what qualifies God to be all deserving of our honor. When it comes to honoring others, that doesn't mean quite the same as honoring God, because God is deserving of the highest honor. When we honor others we acknowledge who they are as a person, we show kindness to them, and we show humility to them. So living an honorable life looks like two things: (1) choosing to recognize and give praise to God for all He has done, and (2) choosing to respect others out of the love of Christ.

What does honor mean to you?

_____

_____

_____

_____

Along with honoring the Lord we are to honor one another.
What does it mean to honor one another?

_____

_____

_____

_____

_____

We are told in different parts of the Bible that God will honor us.
What does that mean to you?

_____

_____

_____

_____

_____

Name some ways in which you can honor the Lord.

_____

_____

_____

_____

_____

_____

_____

Look up the verses and write them in the space below:

Proverbs 3:9

1 Corinthians 6:19-20

Romans 12:10

Choose one of the ways to honor God that you wrote down in response to the questions on the previous pages. Do more research on it, look it up in the Bible, and journal about how you can work to honor God more in that area of your life below:

Friend

No longer do I call you servants, for the servant does not know what his master is doing; but I have called you friends, for all that I have heard from my Father I have made known to you.

JOHN 15:15 ESV

A FRIEND IS SOMEONE YOU ENJOY BEING WITH.

Jesus calls us His friends, which means that He enjoys being with us. Jesus is truly the ultimate friend. Our earthly friends are amazing, and we need community, but friends can let us down and we can let our friends down too. Our friends can sometimes hurt us or say things they don't truly mean. Friendships are hard, but they are always worth fighting for because God created us to be in community with one another. Yet God will never let us down. He speaks life into us through His Word constantly. His Spirit is always with us no matter where we go or what we do. The way in which Jesus is a friend to us is how we should try to be a friend to others. While Jesus was on this earth, He modeled for us what it looks like to be a good friend. We are to love our friends with no end, put their needs above our own, extend grace and forgiveness, and walk through life encouraging each other.

What does it mean to be a friend?

_____

_____

What are the qualities you want in a friendship?

In what ways do you feel that you are a good friend?

What is something you can work on to be a better friend?

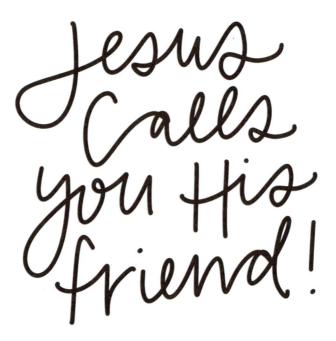

WHAT DOES THAT MEAN TO YOU?

Think of a friend you love dearly. What are some qualities about them that you admire? Write them a card or send them a text thanking them for their friendship. Journal about the experience below.

Chosen

You are a chosen people, a royal priesthood, a holy nation, God's special possession, that you may declare the praises of Him who called you out of darkness into His wonderful light.

I PETER 2:9 NIV

TO BE CHOSEN IS TO BE SELECTED OR MARKED FOR FAVOR.

God chose us to be here on this earth for this time. We seem to be a people always in search of our purpose. It can be easy to spiral, thinking that our life doesn't have meaning or purpose. But those thoughts are false! Each of us was created to live during this exact time and place to fulfill God's amazing plans for our lives. It's so easy to caught up in the busyness of life, running from one task to the next, never finding time to think through why we are doing the things we do. We can even start to believe that our lives are just one to-do after the next. But the truth is, we are a chosen people! When God created you in your mother's womb, He was choosing you to be alive right now. Before you were even born you were already chosen. Your purpose was set before you before you even knew or understood what purpose was. God chose you specifically to live out the life you are in right now. It truly is something to rejoice in and be thankful for. Even if we may not feel "chosen" by the people around us all the time, we are continually chosen by Christ.

What does it mean to you to be chosen?

When you think about the fact that God chose you specifically to be on earth right now, how does that make you feel?

God doesn't have to choose us, but He does because He loves us. What is something you choose to do that you don't have to?

What has God chosen you to walk in right now? What season of life are you currently in?

"IN HIM WE ARE ALSO chosen HAVING BEEN PREDESTINED ACCORDING TO THE PLAN OF HIM WHO WORKS OUT everything IN CONFORMITY WITH THE PURPOSE OF HIS WILL."

ephesians 1:11

Write a prayer below giving thanks to God for choosing you.

Treasure

For where your treasure is, there your heart will be also.

MATTHEW 6:21 NIV

TREASURE IS A THING OR PERSON THAT HAS GREAT VALUE OR IS HIGHLY PRIZED.

What do you consider your treasures? What are the things that you truly value in life? What are the things you place your worth in? Do you place your value and worth on your title at work? your degree? your bank account? your talents and abilities? your beauty? In today's world, it seems we are told that if we make more money, have a better job, and have a social media following, then we will be rich in the terms of the world. But those things are fleeting. They are the kind of treasures that can be taken away in an instant. The kind of treasure our hearts are truly longing for is Jesus and all He has to offer us. Heaven itself is the ultimate treasure. Eternal life seated right next to God is where are treasures should be. It is hard to believe, though, when we can't see it. But if we continue to place our value on temporary, earthly things, it can distract us from the ultimate treasure. Place all your treasure in the Lord and who He is, and the reward will be eternal rather than something that could be gone tomorrow.

What does treasure mean to you?

Where are you storing your treasure today? Why there?

_____

_____

_____

_____

_____

Is it hard for you to believe the true treasure that is for you in Jesus? Why or why not?

_____

_____

_____

_____

_____

The Bible says, "For where your treasure is, there your heart will be also." Where do you feel like your heart is right now?

_____

_____

_____

_____

_____

_____

Trace the verse below:

"BUT LAY UP FOR YOURSELVES treasures IN HEAVEN."
Matthew 6:20

Is there something you put your value in that could be taken away tomorrow? Write about it and ask God to help you release that treasure and grab on more tightly to the treasure that He is.

Content

Not that I was ever in need, for I have learned how to be content with whatever I have. I know how to live on almost nothing or with everything. I have learned the secret of living in every situation, whether it is with a full stomach or empty, with plenty or little.

PHILIPPIANS 4:11-12 NLT

TO BE CONTENT IS TO BE SATISFIED WITH WHAT YOU HAVE.

It is so hard to stay content in life. We are constantly told that to be content we must have more, which is a vicious cycle. If we always feel like we need more, then we will never be truly satisfied. Our posessions will never satisfy us; only Jesus can. We can trust that He will always provide for us what we need. That doesn't always mean He will give us what we want in life. The secret to a full life is contentment, and that means being satisfied if you have very little or if you have plenty. The way to true contentment is to be satisfied with God and God alone, nothing else. We are told many times in the Bible that we will be taken care of, so we truly have nothing to worry about when we place our trust fully in Jesus. What He provides for us may not be exactly what we want, but it will be exactly what we need. And in the end, He is the one who truly satisfies us. He alone is all we need.

What does it mean to you to be content?

_____

_____

_____

_____

Do you feel like you are in a place of contentment right now or a place of dissatisfaction? How does it feel to be in this place?

_____

_____

_____

_____

What are some things you may need to release control of in order to be content?

_____

_____

_____

_____

Do you feel like it's hard for you to trust that the Lord will provide your every need? Why or why not?

_____

_____

_____

_____

be content in All things
be content in All things
be content in All things
be content in All things
be content in All things
be content in All things
be content in All things

What is an area in your life that's hard for you to find contentment in? Reach out to a friend or someone at your church to tell them about this area and ask for prayer over it. Journal about your experience below.

Refine

You rejoice in this, even though now for a short time, if necessary, you suffer grief in various trials so that the proven character of your faith—more valuable than gold which, though perishable, is refined by fire—may result in praise, glory, and honor at the revelation of Jesus Christ.

I PETER 1:6-7 CSB

TO BE REFINED IS TO BE FREE FROM IMPURITIES.

Just as gold is refined by fire to be rid of imperfections and impurities, we too are to be refined by the fire—fire meaning the trials we will go through. Through our grief and our suffering, our faith is refined and strengthened. Through the hardships and trials, we are to walk side by side with Jesus. He endured the harshest suffering of all, dying for us so that we would have the ability to be freed from our impurities. Since He walked through the fire before us, we can trust that He will bring us through the fire as well, brighter and better than before. The trials we face here on earth are hard; the grief, loss, and suffering can be very difficult. We can take heart through them all, though, because we know who has overcome the world. Our time here on earth is so small compared to the life ahead of us in eternity at the right hand of God. As we walk through fire here on earth, we are being refined into who God has made us to be and are preparing ourselves for eternity in heaven with Him.

What does it mean to be refined?

What trials or "fires" are you walking through right now?

As we are being refined, we begin to look more like Jesus. What are some things you have learned about Jesus through your trials?

To be refined is a scary thing, but the outcome of it is so beautiful. Jot down some of your thoughts about being refined.

WE CAN CHOOSE
TO LET OUR TRIALS
define US OR
refine US.

We are going to have trials and troubles in this world.
We can choose to let them define us or refine us. Where do you find
yourself right now with your life's trials? What are steps you can take
to move from a place of feeling defined by your trials to being refined
by them?

mercy

Let us then approach God's throne of grace with confidence, so that we may receive mercy and find grace to help us in our time of need.

TO HAVE MERCY IS TO SHOW SOMEONE KINDNESS OR FORGIVENESS WHEN THEY ARE DESPERATE OR MAY NOT BE DESERVING OF IT.

The Lord is so merciful. He freely extends to us His kindness and forgiveness even though we are not deserving of it. Truly His mercy is one of the most beautiful qualities about Him. We go against His Word, our nature is sinful, we were born into a corrupt world, yet He sent His Son to save us so that we could be free from our sin and live with Him in eternity. His mercy is never ending and never ceasing. It is something that we can always cry out for, and He will be right there to give it. Just as God is merciful to us, we are to be merciful to others, but it can be really hard. Extending kindness and forgiveness after someone has turned away from us or done something to hurt us is not our first response. But because God is rich in mercy and we want to do everything we can to look more like Him, we too are to put on mercy. Wear kindness on your sleeve and freely give away forgiveness out of your love for the Lord. In His strength you can put on the quality of mercy. And in the times that you fail, His ultimate mercy will be right there waiting for you.

What does mercy mean to you?

How have you experienced God's loving mercy?

How can you begin to extend the mercy that He shows you to others?

What makes it hard to extend mercy to others?

"As for you, O Lord, you will not restrain your mercy from me; your steadfast love and your faithfulness will ever preserve me."

psalm 40:11

In the Bible, Jesus said during His sermon on the mount, "Blessed are the merciful, for they will be shown mercy" (Matthew 5:7 NIV). Those who show mercy will be shown mercy. How is God calling you to show mercy today? Journal about it below.

Noble

Finally, brothers and sisters, whatever is true, whatever is noble, whatever is right, whatever is pure, whatever is lovely, whatever is admirable—if anything is excellent or praiseworthy—think about such things.

PHILIPPIANS 4:8 NIV

TO BE NOBLE IS TO POSSESS OUTSTANDING QUALITIES.

God does not want us to worry but instead to think about things that are noble. He longs for us to give Him our concerns and to fill our thoughts with things that are outstanding and excellent. Jesus embodies what it means to be noble. He is outstanding in every way. He is wise, He is a leader, He is humble in heart, and He is pure excellence and perfection. This verse calls us to think of what is noble because Jesus is the ultimate noble one. He is what we are to be thinking about. His kingdom is to be our mindset. The more we think about Him, the more we know Him, and the more we become like Him. When negative and harsh thoughts flood our minds, we can interrupt them with the thought of who He is. We aren't called to be noble because we can never truly be excellent and outstanding. But rather we become more noble as we think about the One who is.

What does noble mean to you?

_____

_____

_____

_____

Describe how Jesus is noble.

_____

_____

_____

_____

What does the verse above mean to you?

_____

_____

_____

Is it easy or hard for you to think of things that are noble? Why do you think that is?

_____

_____

_____

_____

Write down things that are noble to think about.

Noble things to think about:

-
-
-
-
-

When your thoughts begin to consume you, come back to this page and read about the things you believe to be noble. Think about these things. Why did you name the things on the previous page as noble? Write about it below.

Faith

He replied, "Because you have so little faith. Truly I tell you, if you have faith as small as a mustard seed, you can say to this mountain, 'Move from here to there,' and it will move. Nothing will be impossible for you."

MATTHEW 17:20 NIV

TO HAVE FAITH IS TO BELIEVE AND TRUST IN GOD.

Jesus tells us that even faith as tiny as a mustard seed can move mountains. That is truly how powerful it is to have faith in who God is and what He is capable of. A mustard seed's average size is 2.5mm. That is the amount of faith that Jesus asks us to have. Yet so often we can begin to doubt God and try to take control of things on our own. If we try to have faith in man or even in our own selves, we will constantly be let down. But if we have true faith in God, faith in His promises and who He says He is to us, we will see miracles, experience His presence, and overcome the trials and hardships in front of us. We can trust Him. His Word is the truth, and it will never fail us. We can have full faith that the Lord will fulfill His promises to us. We can have full faith that the Lord knows what is best for our lives. And we can have full faith that the Lord will never leave us all the days of our lives.

What does it mean to have faith?

_____

_____

_____

_____

What circumstances make it hard for you to have faith?

_____

_____

_____

_____

What circumstances make it easy for you to have faith?

_____

_____

_____

_____

What is a step you can take today to have mustard seed faith?

_____

_____

_____

_____

even faith as
tiny as a mustard
seed can move
mountains

What are some things you are facing that you need defeated? What mountains stand in your way? What things are you needing God to fully take care of? Write them below and declare your trust and faith in Him over those things today.

Glory

When the Son of Man comes in His glory, and all the angels with Him, He will sit on His glorious throne.

MATTHEW 25:31 NIV

TO GIVE GLORY IS TO ADORE, PRAISE, OR GIVE WORSHIPFUL THANKSGIVING TO SOMEONE OR SOMETHING. TO EMBODY GLORY IS TO BE MAGNIFICENT OR SHINE WITH BEAUTY.

The Lord is glorious, and because of His glory, He deserves to be glorified in all ways. The Lord our God is truly magnificent. He is perfect and excellent in every way. Because of who He is and what He has done for us, He deserves to be praised all the days of our lives. His love, His grace, His mercy, His peace, His compassion, and His joy are a few of the things that make Him more than worthy of our praise and thanksgiving. Imagine the day that the Lord comes back to earth. His glory will be undeniable, but not only will it be undeniable then, it is just as undeniable now. He gives us glimpses of His glory through people and experiences. He Himself is the definition of glory, and if His presence is with us everywhere, then so is His glory. Let us give continual thanks and worship to Him who is more than deserving of our glory, honor, and praise.

What does glory mean to you?

What makes God glorious to you?

In what ways has God's glory impacted your life?

What are ways that you can give God the glory and praise He deserves?

Trace the saying below over and over and hold it in your heart:

HE IS DESERVING
OF ALL
honor
AND
glory
AND
praise

What is an active step you can take today to glorify God?
(Maybe you take time to worship Him, maybe it looks like writing
a gratitude list, maybe it looks like praying to Him and thanking Him
for who He is.) Whatever it is you choose to do, take five minutes to
glorify God and then write about the experience below.

Enough

He said to me, "My grace is sufficient for you, for My power is perfected in weakness." Therefore, I will most gladly boast all the more about my weaknesses, so that Christ's power may reside in me.

II CORINTHIANS 12:9-10 CSB

TO BE ENOUGH IS TO BE SUFFICIENT FOR A PURPOSE OR TO SATISFY A DESIRE.

The only thing that can ever fully satisfy our deepest desire to be known or loved is the love and presence of God. Christ is enough for us, and in Him we are enough. On our own, we aren't enough. We were created to need our Savior. The emptiness or dissatisfaction we may feel is our human flesh in desperate need of a Savior. The love and acceptance we try to find in the world will never be enough for us because what we need is who Jesus is. His grace alone is enough for us. In our weakness, we are desperate for His grace. He meets us in our weakness and our brokenness and gives us His power. How beautiful is it that we are enough as we are because of the beautiful grace of God? He doesn't expect us to do anything to earn His grace other than just say yes to Him. He will fill us to overflowing. We are enough in the One who is more than enough for us.

What does it mean to you to be enough?

_____

_____

Have you ever felt like you had to do certain things or be a certain way to "be enough" for someone? Explain.

_____

_____

_____

_____

_____

Christ is enough for you. Because of who He is and the grace He lavishes upon you, you are enough. What does that mean to you?

_____

_____

_____

_____

_____

What makes Christ enough for you? Name the things below.

_____

_____

_____

_____

_____

_____

on our own we
are not enough
BUT by Him +
in His grace,
He makes us
enough.

You are free to release the pressure of trying to be enough for someone or for the world. Christ has already declared you enough for Him just as you are. Journal your feelings about that below.

Refreshed

Therefore if anyone is in Christ [that is, grafted in, joined to Him by faith in Him as Savior], *he is a new creature* [reborn and renewed by the Holy Spirit]; *the old things* [the previous moral and spiritual condition] *have passed away. Behold, new things have come* [because spiritual awakening brings a new life].

II CORINTHIANS 5:17 AMP

TO BE REFRESHED IS TO BE MADE NEW.

Christ is our refresher. He makes us new through His Spirit. In Him our spirits are renewed, our minds and hearts are refreshed, and we are made a new creation. Being in His presence is one of the most refreshing experiences. In His presence is fullness of joy, in His presence is where we learn about who He is, and in His presence is where we become refreshed. There are many pictures in the Bible that show us how refreshing God truly is. He makes us lie down in green pastures and leads us beside still waters (Psalm 23:2). He clothes the lilies in the fields (Matthew 6:30). He wants to bring refreshment to our lives. He is at work refreshing you and making you new in Him. When we say yes to Him, our old self is put away and a new self is in the making—one that has been forgiven, set free, and fully refreshed in who the Father is.

What does it mean to you to be refreshed?

How have you seen God bring refreshment in your life?

What makes God refreshing to you?

Who is someone that is refreshing to you? What makes them refreshing? (Text them and tell them!)

What is a place that is refreshing to you? Describe it and draw it below.

A refreshing place:

Write a prayer below thanking God for His refreshing presence.

Dwell

Surely goodness and mercy shall follow me all the days of my life,
*and I shall dwell in the house of the L*ORD *forever.*

PSALM 23:6 ESV

TO DWELL IS TO REMAIN IN SOMETHING.

When we dwell with God, we are remaining with Him. Dwelling with the Lord is choosing to be conscious of His presence among us. In the verse above, when we read that we shall "dwell in the house of the Lord forever," it means we get to live life while soaking in God's love every day. His presence is always around us and always with us. In this fast-paced world we live in, it is easy to become distracted and forget that fact. When we lose sight of His presence, we can begin to dwell on worries and concerns and not on the true promises of God. Being aware of His presence daily and having a mindset of dwelling in the Lord is life changing. His presence is what molds and shapes us into who we are meant to be. Dwelling in the house of the Lord is one of the greatest decisions we can make on this side of heaven.

What does it mean to you to dwell?

_____

_____

_____

_____

What does it look like to you to dwell in the house of the Lord?

What makes it hard to dwell in His presence?

Do you find yourself craving rest? Why do you think we are people who need and crave rest?

"surely goodness and mercy shall follow me all the days of my life, and I shall dwell in the house of the lord forever."

psalm 23:6

What are steps you can take to choose to dwell in His presence daily?
What are things you can implement into your daily routine or things
you can take out to be able to dwell with Him constantly?

Truth

Jesus answered, "I am the way and the truth and the life. No one comes to the Father except through me."

JOHN 14:6 NIV

TRUTH IS A VERIFIED OR INDISPUTABLE FACT.

In this verse Jesus defines Himself as the truth. There is nothing indisputable about who Jesus is. There is no lie or deceitfulness in His promises. The only way to the Father and eternal life is to believe fully in who Jesus is and how He has taught us to live. The promises that Jesus has for us are beautiful. They are what our hearts yearn for. We need Jesus, therefore we need truth—but not the kind of truth that is twisted to fit our desires and wants, rather the truth that is written in the Bible, unchanged and everlasting. The truth that Jesus calls us to walk in can be hard. Sometimes the truth in the Bible doesn't line up with what is cool or what's popular. But that is actually the whole point. Following and walking in the truth isn't going to be easy. It is going to be hard, but it will be radically life changing and carries with it the promise of eternal life seated next to the Father in heaven.

What does truth mean to you?

_____

_____

_____

What are some "truths" that the world has made you believe that don't line up with what the Bible actually says?

Why do you feel it is hard to stand in truth sometimes?

When you hear Jesus call Himself the truth, what does that mean to you?

Your truth
is NOT
as powerful
as THE
truth.

—Sadie Robertson Huff

Think about different ways you can actively stand in truth (e.g., memorizing Scripture, reading the Word every morning, having quotes on your mirror that remind you of truth). Journal about some different ways that can help you have truth written on your heart every day.

So in Christ Jesus you are all children of God through faith, for all of you who were baptized into Christ have clothed yourselves with Christ. There is neither Jew nor Gentile, neither slave nor free, nor is there male and female, for you are all one in Christ Jesus.

GALATIANS 3:26-28 NIV

IDENTITY DEFINES WHO OR WHAT A PERSON OR THING IS.

Our true identity that defines who we are is in the fact that we are children of God. There are many things that can make us believe our identity is here on earth. It can be easy to place it in the things that we do. Some of us are students, teachers, nurses, doctors, creatives, mentors, achievers, introverts, and the list can go on and on. But the things that we do don't define our true identity. Yes, those things make up who we are and can be beautiful gifts that the Lord has blessed us with, but they are temporary. Our identity as children of the living God is eternal and can never be taken away from us. The second we said yes to Him and yes to faith, we were clothed in who He is. Walk confidently in your identity as a beautiful and beloved child of God.

What does identity mean to you?

What are some earthly things you have found your identity in?

_____

_____

_____

_____

_____

_____

Why is it hard sometimes to believe in our true identity as children of God?

_____

_____

_____

_____

_____

_____

What are ways you can begin to walk in your identity as a child of God?

_____

_____

_____

_____

_____

_____

_____

Write down all the things that you believe to be your identity or that you place your identity in on the left side (for example, status, money, job title, etc.). Then on the right side write down identities that are never fleeting.

False
identities:

ex: my job

·

·

·

·

·

True
identities:

ex: daughter of
christ

·

·

·

·

·

Text a friend an encouraging note letting them know that they are a beloved child of God and nothing can take that identity away from them. Journal about the experience below.

Intentional

For you formed my inward parts; you knitted me together in my mother's womb. I praise you, for I am fearfully and wonderfully made. Wonderful are your works; my soul knows it very well.

PSALM 139: 13–14 ESV

TO BE INTENTIONAL IS TO DO SOMETHING WITH PURPOSE.

The Lord was intentional when He made you because He made you with great purpose. He was intentional in how He created the universe; He is intentional in choosing when certain things happen; He is intentional in giving us His gifts. Truly everything He does is done with beautiful intent and purpose. He does that so we can taste and see how good He is and how much He really does love us. He is intentional in His love for us, showing it to us in ways that each of us individually need. He chooses to speak to us in specific ways, knowing that the purpose in it gives us hope and deeper faith in Him. He withholds things from us out of love and with intent. He gives us beautiful things that we don't deserve out of love and with intent. He deserves all the praise and glory for how intentional He is with us.

What does it mean to you to be intentional?

172

Name a few ways in which you have seen and felt God be intentional with you.

_____

_____

_____

_____

_____

What are ways we can be intentional with others?

_____

_____

_____

_____

_____

When someone is intentional with you, what does it make you feel?

_____

_____

_____

_____

_____

_____

_____

Trace the saying below and hold it in your heart today.

He leads us
on His perfect
path for His
perfect purpose.

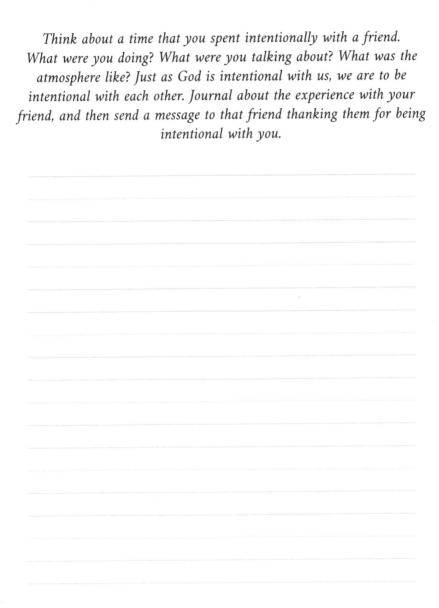

Think about a time that you spent intentionally with a friend. What were you doing? What were you talking about? What was the atmosphere like? Just as God is intentional with us, we are to be intentional with each other. Journal about the experience with your friend, and then send a message to that friend thanking them for being intentional with you.

Restore

He makes me lie down in green pastures. He leads me beside still waters. He restores my soul. He leads me in paths of righteousness for his name's sake.

PSALM 23:2–3 ESV

TO RESTORE SOMETHING IS TO BRING IT BACK TO ITS ORIGINAL STATE OR CONDITION.

The Lord is the ultimate restorer. He takes all our broken pieces, all our mess, and He puts it all back together. But not just how it used to be—no, He makes it even better and more beautiful than before. When our souls are tired, when we feel weary, when we feel broken beyond repair, He comes in and brings the ultimate restoration that we need and long for. He extends to us His peace, His love, His grace, and His compassion. All those things, along with who He is to begin with, are what restore us and bring us to a place of embodying and embracing all of who we are. He brings peace to the chaos, He brings grace to the mess, He brings love to the unlovable, and He shines His light in the dark places. In the quiet, in the busyness, in every day and every season He is restoring your soul.

What does the word restore mean to you?

_____

_____

When you read in the verse above "He restores my soul," what does that make you feel?

What are some areas in your life you feel need to be restored?

What are some things of this world that need to be restored? Pray restoration over those things.

Trace the quote below and believe it over yourself today.

When our soul is tired, when we feel weary, when we feel broken beyond repair, He comes in and brings the ultimate restoration that we need and long for.

Think of a time when you felt restored.
Journal about the experience below.

Refuge

God is our refuge and strength [mighty and impenetrable], a very present and well-proved help in trouble.

PSALM 46:1 AMP

A REFUGE IS A PLACE OF SHELTER OR PROTECTION.

God is our safe place and our protection. He is always with us, watching over us and shielding us from evil. We can trust in Him to provide shelter for us when we need it. He only wants what is best for His children. He desires safety and security for us. He has the true power to do anything because of His might and authority. When we think of refuge, often we think about a place where we can hide, such as a building or place meant to shield from harm. But when it comes to God as our refuge, it is just who He is. He is the safe place. He is where we run for safety when we need protection. He loves when His children's first reaction is to come to Him. In His arms is the safest place we could ever be. He leads us on His perfect path for our life, guiding and protecting us along the way.

What does refuge mean to you?

Is it hard for you to view God as your refuge? Why or why not?

Is there a place (an actual building or area) where you feel safe? Why do you feel safe there?

Is there a person in your life who is like a refuge to you? What is it about them that makes you feel safe?

Describe or draw your safe place in the space below.

my safe space
looks like:

Reach out to the friend that you wrote about in question 4. Let them know that they make you feel safe. Write about the experience below.

Goodness

But the Holy Spirit produces this kind of fruit in our lives: love, joy, peace, patience, kindness, goodness, faithfulness, gentleness, and self-control. There is no law against these things!

GALATIANS 5:22-23 NLT

GOODNESS IS MORAL EXCELLENCE. IT IS THE QUALITY OF DOING WHAT IS RIGHT AND AVOIDING WHAT IS WRONG.

Jesus embodied moral excellence. He was always choosing what was good and staying away from the things that were not good. The fruits of the Spirit listed above in the verse are characteristics that Jesus displayed and that we are to put on. When we put on goodness, we are choosing to do what is good, what is kind, and what is righteous in the eyes of Christ. There are a lot of things in this world that can seem "good" but actually can be unhealthy for our spirit and wrong to choose to partake in. When it comes to defining things as good, we must ask for guidance from the Lord to help us decipher what is good and what isn't. He desires for us to walk in goodness and to experience His goodness. His goodness will follow us all the days of our lives (Psalm 23:6).

What does goodness mean to you?

What are some things of this world that can seem good but aren't?

How does the goodness of God encourage and inspire you to produce goodness in your own life?

What are ways you can walk and produce the fruit of goodness today?

"SURELY *goodness* AND *mercy* SHALL FOLLOW ME ALL THE DAYS OF MY LIFE, AND I SHALL DWELL IN THE HOUSE OF THE LORD FOREVER."

psalm 23:6

In what areas in your life have you seen and experienced the goodness of God? Journal about those experiences below and thank God for His goodness to you.

In the same way, let your light shine before others, so that they may see your good works and give glory to your Father who is in heaven.

MATTHEW 5:16 ESV

TO IGNITE SOMETHING IS TO SET IT ON FIRE.

The Lord wants our souls to be on fire for Him. He ignites within us the desire to know Him, and He wants us to go out and ignite others. When we know Him and begin to live a life that reflects who He is, our light shines. His light lives within us and is undeniable. It is not our own light that shines but His. He is the light of the world, and we are His shining lights living for Him in all that we do. All He wants is for us to yearn for more of Him, for our souls to be set ablaze and fully consumed with who He is. When we are on fire for Jesus, His light will shine through us to others. Others will notice that light within us and want to know more about it. We are called through the Great Commission to go and make disciples (Matthew 28:19). It is the light that the Lord shines through us that ignites others and sets a fire within them to want to know Jesus more.

What does ignite mean to you?

Where do you feel you are right now in your walk with Jesus? Is your heart on fire for Him, or do you feel like that fire is dim right now?

What does it mean to you to have the light of Christ within you?

What is a way you can let your light shine before others today?

Write out the places and circumstances in your life where you want to let His light shine:

let His light shine
in these places :

- .

- .

- .

- .

- .

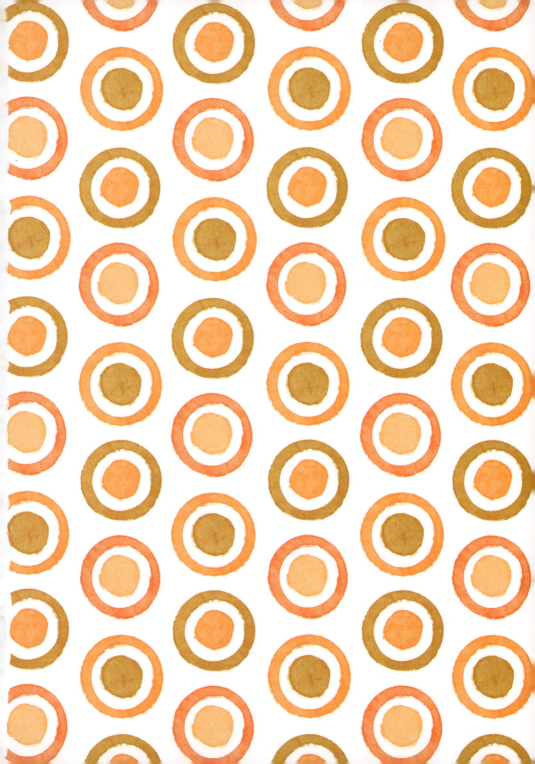

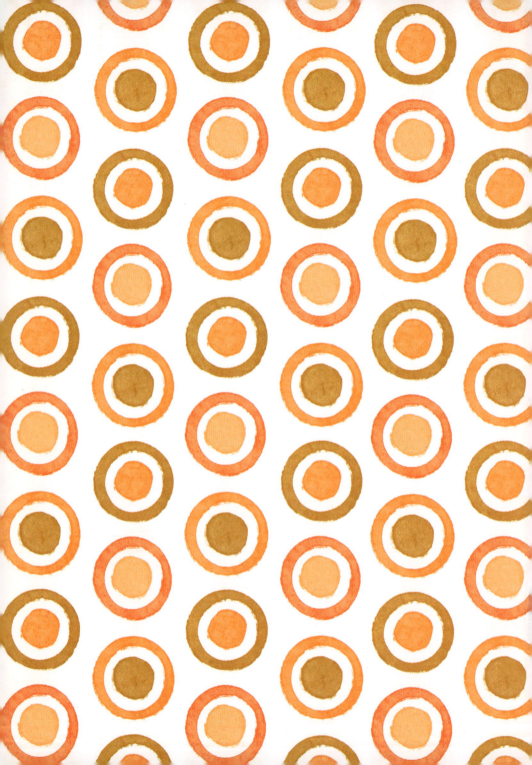

Where is an area in your life you can work on letting your light shine? Maybe it's your workplace, your church, your community, or your gym. What are ways you can let your light shine out to others? How can you begin to ignite in others a desire to know Jesus more? Journal your thoughts below.